Animals of Africa

For Kids

Amazing Animal Books for Young Readers

by Steve Muturi & John Davidson

Read More Amazing Animal Books

Purchase at Amazon.com

Table of Contents

ANIMALS OF EAST AFRICA

East Africa is comprised of Kenya, Uganda, Tanzania, Rwanda and Burundi. The terrain in these countries presents a variety of habitats for wildlife; from arid semi-desert to savannah grasslands to tropical rainforests and snow-capped mountains. As one would expect, the wildlife in the region is varied and plentiful.

THE BIG FIVE

A wildlife safari to East Africa is not complete until one has seen the Big Five. "Safari" is a word that originates from the Swahili of East African coast, and means "journey". The term Big Five was originally meant to identify the most dangerous animals to hunt, but today it identifies the animals that are a must-see. One can only shoot them with a camera!

ELEPHANT

The largest land animals on Earth are African elephants. They are larger than Asian elephants and are easily identifiable by their larger ears that look somewhat like the continent of Africa. African elephants live in the mountain forests and savannah grasslands of sub-Saharan Africa

(African Elephant)

Elephant fan their ears to keep their large bodies cool, but sometimes the African heat is too much. They love water and enjoy cooling off by sucking water into their trunks and spraying it over themselves. They then spray their skin with a coating of dust.

An elephant's trunk is actually its nose and a useful limb. It is used for smelling, breathing, trumpeting, drinking, and also for grabbing hings—especially tasty meals.

African elephants, male and female, have tusks. They strip bark from trees with them. Males battle one another for supremacy using their tusks.

Humans find ivory very valuable, and this has led to the killing of many elephants for their tusks. This trade is illegal, but it has not been possible to completely eliminate it. African elephant populations remain endangered.

Elephants eat bark, leaves, roots, grasses and fruit, and they eat a lot! In a single day, an adult elephant can eat more than 300 pounds of food.

(African elephants with their young)

Matriarchal family groups of related females called a herd for elephant families. The oldest and often largest female in the herd, called a matriarch, is the leader. Several individuals with the number depending on terrain and family size, form a herd. Protection and rearing of calves is shared by the whole herd. Between the ages of 13 and 14, males leave the family unit. They may then live with other males or lead solitary lives.

Intelligent animals, elephants have long memories. During dry seasons, this memory helps matriarchs to guide their herds to watering holes that they remember from the past, though they be hundreds of miles away. This has led to the saying "an elephant never forgets." Elephants also display a range of emotions, ranging from grief, joy, anger and play.

BUFALLO

The African buffalo is the only member of the cattle family found wild in East Africa. The African buffalo is erratic by nature. This makes it very dangerous to humans. For this reason, it has never been tamed - unlike the Asian water buffalo.

(African [Cape] Buffalo)

Savannah buffaloes have black or dark brown coats that darken with age. Mature bulls have white circles around their eyes. Females have reddish coats. Calves' coats are red.

The African buffalo has peculiar horns. A characteristic is the horns of the adult bull. These have fused bases which form a "boss", a continuous bone shield. The boss sometimes cannot be penetrated even by a high powered rifle bullet. The distance between the ends of the horns of large bulls is more than one metre.

One of the most effective at foragers is the buffalo. Floodplains and flooded swamps, as well as mountain forests and savannah grasslands, are its usual territory. Favouring habitat with thick foliage, such as reeds and thickets, the African buffalo can also been found in open woods. In regard to area, they are not too demanding, but they need to drink daily. This means they depend on permanent springs of water. The buffalo can live on coarse grasses, much like the Burchell's zebra. Buffalo chomp up pastures and clear them for the more choosy feeders. Using its wide incisor teeth and long tongue, the buffalo eats grass faster than most African herbivores. Flattened or exhausted areas do not interest the African buffalo for long.

Other than human beings, African buffaloes have few natural predators and are adept at defending themselves against, and killing, even lions. Buffalo are however regularly killed by lions, and in some regions, they are the lions' primary food source. A single adult buffalo can only be brought down by a number of lions working together.

RHINO
(White Rhino with young)

Rhino, as rhinoceros is often shortened, is a large herbivore found in East Africa. The White Rhino is the second largest land mammal after the elephant. Both white and black rhinos are found in East Africa, mostly in game reserves and private ranches, where they are closely guarded against poachers.

The white rhinoceros is actually grey in color. The only differences between black and white rhino is that the black rhinoceros has a pointed upper lip while the white rhino has a square lip, and the white rhino is larger, otherwise they are similar in color. Both have two horns on their snouts.

Black rhinos are browsers that get most of their food from eating trees and bushes. They use their lips to grip and pluck leaves and fruit from the branches. White rhinos graze on grasses, walking with their enormous heads and squared lips low to the ground.

Except for females and their offspring, black rhinos are solitary animals. Females reproduce only once every two and a half to five years. The lone calf does not live on its own until it is about three years old.

Rhinos have a keen sense of smell and sharp hearing. They may find one another by following the trail of scent each animal leaves behind it on the landscape. However, their eyesight is poor.

The prominent horn for which rhinos are so well known has also been the cause of their downfall. Many animals have been killed for the hard, hairlike growth, which is revered for medicinal uses in most of Asia. The horn is also a valuable commodity in North Africa and the Middle East as an ornamental dagger handle.

Rhinos have a tough hide that looks like armour plating. The Swahili word for them is "kifaru" and is the same word used for military tanks!

LION

Lions live in groups called prides. They are the only big cat that lives in groups. Comprising of up to three males and a dozen females, and their young, prides are family units and all the lionesses are related. Female cubs usually stay with the group as they grow older. Young males commonly leave the pride and establish their own. They do this by fighting for and taking over another male's family group.

Manes, the impressive fringe of long black or brown hair that surrounds the heads, only occur in males. The family's territory which may include some 100 square miles of savannah grassland, scrub, or open woodlands, is defended by the males. They mark the area with urine and roar menacingly to warn intruders. They and chase off any animals that encroach on their turf.

Hunting is mainly done by the female lions. They kill antelopes, buffalo, zebras, wildebeest, and other big animals in the savannah. The lions work together as a team, as many of these animals are faster than them. Young lions only start hunting after about a year. If the opportunity presents itself, lions may hunt alone. They have also been known to deprive cheetah, hyenas or wild dogs of their kills.

(Lioness with cubs)

The Swahili name for lion is "Simba", which will be familiar to anyone who's ever watched The Lion King.

LEOPARD

The leopard, a feline with a wide range in some parts of East Africa, is facing population decline due to human activity and fragmentation, and hunting for trade, poaching and pest control.

(Snarling leopard)

The leopard is the smallest of the "big cats". Compared to other members of the family, the leopard has comparatively short legs and a long body with a large head. Its fur is marked with distinct closely packed "rosettes". The coat color generally varies from a deep gold to pale yellow or tawny, and it is marked with dark rosettes, which are circular in the East African leopard. The head, lower limbs and stomach have solid black spots. The species' success is somewhat due to its skill as an opportunistic hunter, its adaptability to different habitats and its ability to run fast - at speeds approaching 36 mph. It is unmatched in its ability to climb trees even when carrying a heavy carcass, and it is notorious for stealth. The leopard consumes virtually any animal that it can catch. Its locale ranges from woodlands to rainforest to desert terrains.

Leopards are solitary, elusive and generally nocturnal. Leopards often hunt from up in trees - the speckled coats make them virtually invisible until the final deadly spring. By stealth, these nocturnal predators also track antelope and warthogs. When human settlements are present, leopards often attack dogs and, sometimes, people.

(Leopard with cub)

Breeding happens all year round. Two grayish cubs with faintly visible spots are born. The cubs are hidden by the mother, and often moved from one safe hiding place to the next until they are old enough to begin learning to hunt. The mothers keep the cubs with them for about two years.

OTHER ANIMALS OF INTEREST IN EAST AFRICA

WILDEBEESTE
(Wildebeeste)

The gnu, an awkward-looking large member of the antelope family, earned the Afrikaans name wildebeest, or "wild beast," for the funny looking appearance with its big head, mane, beard, and sharp curved horns. The wildebeest is a source of food for the other predators of the Africa: wild dogs, lions, leopards, and hyenas.

Their territory covers the grassy savannah plains and open woodlands of eastern Africa, particularly the Serengeti in Tanzania and Masai Mara in Kenya. They travel in large herds and are diurnal, grazing continually.

The wildebeests' spectacular annual migration in search of greener pastures is dictated by weather, but usually takes place in May or June and the return leg around October. It is one of the greatest wildlife spectacles on Earth. The migration involves up to 1.5 million wildebeeste, with hundreds of thousands of other animals, including zebra, tagging along.

Up to half a million calves are born in February and March each year, at the beginning of the rainy season. Calves can usually walk within minutes of birth and can run around after a short time. The calves are able to keep up with the herd within a few days. Gnus live for around 20 years.

ZEBRA

An member of the horse family from Africa, zebras are
distinguishable by their stripes. Their stripes come in diverse forms
but each individual has a matchless pattern. Generally communal
animals, zebras that live in medium-sized herds. Zebras have never
been truly domesticated, not like their closest kin, donkeys and
horses.

(Grevy's zebra)

Plains (Burchell's) zebra and Grevy's are the two species found in
East Africa.

Zebras are one of the animals most familiar to people. This is because
of their unique stripes. They occur in a range of territories such as
horny scrublands, woodlands, coastal hills, savannah grasslands and
mountains.

It was believed that zebras had white hides with black stripes, as some
zebras have white underbellies. However, research has shown that the
zebra's hide is black in color and the white stripes and bellies are add-

ons.

The zebra's main body, head, forequarters and neck have vertical stripes, and there are level stripes on the legs and rear. The zebra's black and white stripes gave the name to the "zebra crossing" on roads.

IMPALA

Impalas are elegant, graceful smallish antelopes that roam the savannah and light woodlands of eastern and southern Africa. They usually appear in herds of hundreds, browsing on shoots, grasses, shrubs, herbs and bushes and only when food is abundant, like during the rainy season.

(Male impala)

Herding offers individuals protection from predators like lions and cheetah. It only takes one watchful impala to give a cry that sets the entire herd running - and a bolting impala is not easy to catch.

Impalas can run very fast runners and are able to leap expanses beyond 30 feet. They use their leaping ability evade predators. At times, it seems, they leap around for fun. The impala can also leap over bushy shrubs and other hurdles by leaping some 10 feet in the air. Usually, a running impala will simply take a flying leap over anything in its path.

It's long, spiralling horns make this graceful antelope distinctive.

Males use their horns to challenge each other in tests of strength and dominance. Older impala males claim mating ranges and gather groups of females that they protectively guard against any challengers. During the fatiguing breeding time, the male must fight off challengers, guard his females, and mate with them. Unsuccessful challenges to a male's territory usually end with the loser retreating to join a herd of bachelor impala.

Females usually give birth about seven months after they mate, usually to a single offspring. Both mother and baby join the herd of other females and offspring within a few days.

GIRAFFE

The giraffe is the tallest living animal on Earth, and the largest ruminant. Its name comes from the fact that it looks like a camel and the patches of color on its fur. It has a very long neck and legs, it also has horns that look like knobs on the top of its head.

(Giraffes)

Giraffes usually live in the grasslands, and open woodlands. Their primary food source is acacia leaves, because of their long necks they can reach up into the trees for food. The giraffe's tongue is also long! The tongue, which can grow to more than 20 inches, enables them to eat leaves and buds from twigs, twisting between the sharp acacia horns. Giraffes are preyed on by lions. Calves are also hunted by spotted hyenas, wild dogs and leopards. Adults do not make strong social bonds. They do sometimes gather in loose groups if they happen to be going the same way. Males establish social relationships through "necking". They have fights, using the head and neck as a weapon. Males fight for dominance so they can mate with the females. Females raise the young by themselves.

Most human beings are shorter than the giraffe's legs alone! These 6 foot plus legs make it possible for giraffes to run fast. They do as much as 35 miles an hour over short distances and can also attain 15 miles an hour for longer distances.

A giraffe is able to watch for predators across the wide African savanna because of its great height. However, it is sometimes disadvantageous to be so tall because it makes difficult and dangerous for a giraffe to drink water. Giraffes are forced to extend their legs out wide and bend all the way down in a difficult position, which exposes to attack by predators like Africa's big cats. Giraffes get most of their water from the succulent plants they eat, so they only need to drink once every several days.

Female giraffes give birth standing. The 1.5-metre-or-more fall to the ground at birth introduces the young giraffes to the world in a rather rough way. It only takes the infants half an hour or so to stand on their feet, and within ten hours of birth they can run with their mothers.

Giraffes have beautiful spotted skins. No two individuals have exactly the same pattern. However, giraffes from the same region appear similar.

GERENUK

The gerenuk is a member of the antelope family. It has an elongated neck and is found in arid thorn bush and semi-desert in East Africa. The word gerenuk is Somali for "giraffe-necked". It is also known as Waller's gazelle.

(Gerenuk)

Gerenuks have a small head compared to the body, but their eyes and ears are proportionally large. Horns are only present in males. Their necks are also more muscular than those of females. The coats of both sexes are reddish brown. Their tails are short and black-tipped. The gerenuk's long thin neck is its distinguishing identifier. The neck can be extended further for feeding from the woodland undergrowth and tall bushes of the desert. The gerenuk's long slender legs are another advantage, as they allow it to run away very fast when a predator threatens. Breeders say the gerenuk is very humble. In African tribal tales, the gerenuk is often called 'Queen of Humility.'

Gerenuks hardly ever graze. They prefer to feed from bushes and acacia trees. They stand erect on their rear legs and stretch their necks, which enables them to reach higher branches and twigs than other grazers. They prefer the more succulent leaves and shoots, but they also eat fruit, buds, flowers, and herbs. Gerenuks get enough water from the plants they eat; they don't need to drink. This enables them to can survive in very dry areas. Lions, cheetahs, jackals and leopards are the gerenuk's main predators.

WARTHOG
(A warthog)

The warthog is a member of the pig family, found in open and lightly forested areas of Africa. The animal is a thinly haired, large-headed, blackish or brown animal standing about 30 inches tall at the shoulder. It has a bristly mane extending from the neck to the middle of the back, and it has a long, thin, tail that it carries high when it is alarmed. The male has four bumps, or warts, on its face. The female has two. Both sexes bear tusks; those of the lower jaw are formidable weapons, and those of the upper jaw curve upward and inward in a semicircle, reaching a length of more than 24 inches in some males.

The warthog is a sociable animal that feeds on grass and other foliage. It often feeds while on its knees! It often shelters in anteater burrows, which it enlarges with its tusks and enters backward so as to be able to defend itself with its tusks. In the morning, the warthogs emerge from these borrows at full speed and run in a straight line for more than 20 feet.

The typical pregnancy period is five or six months. When they are about to give birth, sows temporarily leave their families to give birth in a separate hole. The litter is two to eight piglets, with two to four the usual average. The mother will stay in the hole for several weeks tending her piglets. Piglets begin foraging at about two to three weeks and are weaned by six months. Warthog young quickly attain agility and stay close to their mothers for defence.

The warthog's main form of defence is running off at high speeds and dodging around. However, it has a very short memory, and warthogs are often observed to begin grazing placidly mere seconds after evading a lion or leopard!

BABOON
(Baboon)

Baboons are a species of large, robust, and largely land-dwelling monkeys found in dry regions of East Africa. Males of the largest species typically weigh about 66 pounds, but females are only half this size. They have long muzzles with the nostrils located at the end; male baboons have long knife-like canine teeth, which they sometimes display very impressively in a show of aggression.

Unlike most monkeys, which live in tropical forests, baboons are mostly are found in savannah and semiarid regions, where they ramble on the ground. They frequently climb trees, however, and here they sleep, keep lookout, and sometimes feed. Baboons eat a variety of plants and animals, including grass and grass seeds, roots, fruit, pods, and tubers that they dig up. They also eat birds, rodents, and even antelope fawns that they find hiding in long grass. In human villages they are often said to kill lambs and goat kids, and far and wide they are known as destructive crop raiders.

The most common species found in East Africa are the yellow baboon and the olive baboon. Their names refer to the color of their fur, with the olive baboon being an olive-green. These species are often denoted savannah baboons, and they have much in common. All live in large unified troops numbering from 10 to several hundred. Within each troop there is a supremacy competition among adult males. They threaten each other and often fight, and the dominance status is always changing. The dominance order of females is much more stable. Dominant members of each sex have the first choice of favorite foods and mating companions; they also keep order within the group, chasing and threatening underlings that are fighting or otherwise causing disorder.

The alpha male will mate with more females than other males and thus will father a high percentage of the next generation. A single infant is born after a pregnancy of five to six months. The young are clearly black in color and are permitted a great deal of freedom in their manners.

Baboons that have become accustomed to humans can be a nuisance and at times even dangerous. They have been known to rob children of food and males will often harass women and girls. Anyone driving in a baboon zone is advised to roll up all windows and lock the doors!

VILLAGE WEAVERBIRD

Weaverbirds are a number of small finch-like birds that are noted for their prowess in building complex nests using grass and other plant fibers. They are principally well-known for their vaulted nests, which in some African species form intricate, hanging interwoven compartments. Many species of weavers form lively and noisy flocks which can number in the thousands.

Weaver bird Africa, Ploceidae)

The male usually has bright yellow marks, and makes a nest that looks a lot like an upside-down flask, with a bottom entrance, which may be a sort of duct. He attracts females by dangling upside down from the nest while calling and flapping his wings. Females judge the male by how well his nest is built. If she doesn't like the nest, she undoes the knots holding it onto the twig and it falls to the ground – the male then has to start building from scratch!

After mating, 2-3 eggs are laid. The weaver is a colonial breeder, so many nests may hang from one tree.

This often abundant species occurs in a wide range of open locales, including woodlands and human residences, and habitually forms large noisy colonies in towns, villages and hotel grounds.

Village Weavers feed principally on seeds and grains. They and can be a crop pest, but they will gladly take insects, especially when feeding their young, which partially rights the damage to food production.

The calls of this bird include loud chattering and harsh buzzes.

GREATER FLAMINGO

Greater flamingoes usually gather in warm, tropical, boggy regions. These pink birds are found on most continents. They prefer environments like river mouths and alkaline or saline lakes. Flamingoes are good swimmers, but really flourish on the muddy areas where they feed and breed.

Greater flamingo have curved, long necks. Their bills are yellow, tipped with black and bent downwards distinctively. They use these bent bills to feed on small creatures such as fly larvae, plankton and tiny fish. They stand on their long legs in muddy bogs and shallow water and use their webbed feet to stir up the bottom. They then immerse their heads and beaks and suck up mud and water to access the tasty titbits inside. A filter in the flamingo's bill removes food from the water.

(Greater flamingo in flight)

The flamingo's pink color came from shrimp-like crustaceans it eats. Unless their diet is supplemented or food dye added to their feed, the birds pale while in captivity.

Greater flamingoes live in groups called colonies or flocks. There is safety in numbers, an individual which has its head down in the mud is protected by the others. They also breed in colonies. A single egg is laid and the breeding pair take turns incubating it. Young flamingoes are gray when they hatch; they do not turn pink till they are at least two years old. In drought years when pools are dry, flamingoes may not breed.

OSTRICH

The ostrich is flightless. These birds, the world's largest, ramble across the African desert and savannah lands. Ostriches do not drink as their food provides most of the water they need. Males are mostly black with white plumage while females are grey.

(Three Ostriches)

Ostriches, though they cannot fly, are fast, strong runners. They can dash at up to 43 miles an hour and run over distance at 31 miles an hour. An ostrich's powerful long legs can cover 10 to 16 feet in a single pace. These legs can also be terrible weapons. An ostrich's kicks can kill a human or a would-be hunter like a lion. Each two-toed foot has a long, sharp talon.

Ostriches live in flocks that usually contain less than 12 birds. They live in herds maintained by alpha males, which mate with the group's alpha hen. All the eggs are placed dominant hen's nest. Her own eggs are given the center position. The dominant pair take turns incubating the giant eggs, each one of which can weigh the same as 24 chicken eggs!

Ostriches, contrary to popular myth, do not "bury their heads in the sand". The old story probably comes from one of the bird's defensive behaviors. Ostriches, when threatened, lie down and lower their necks to the ground, trying to be less visible. Their feathers blend well with the terrain and it looks like they have their heads buried in the sand.

Ostriches usually eat plants, seeds, insects, roots, lizards, and any other small creatures they find in their sometimes severe surroundings.

MARABOU STORK
(Marabou stork)

A large African bird with a naked pink head and neck, a reddish throat pouch, and a straight beak, the marabou is the biggest stork. It is roughly 5 feet tall with a wingspread of 8 1/2 feet. Its plumage is mainly dark grey and white.

The Marabou Stork breeds in sub-Saharan Africa, in wet and parched habitats, regularly near human settlements, especially garbage dumps. It is at times called "The Undertaker" due to its color, shape and gait.

The marabou is a gregarious colonial bird. In the dry season in Africa, when food is more freely available as the pools dry up and shrink, the marabou builds a tree nest in which two or three eggs are laid.

Marabou storks have increasingly become dependent on human garbage. Hundreds of them can be found around dumpsites in urban areas. Marabous have been seen to consume almost anything that they can swallow, including pieces of metal and shoes. Marabou storks accustomed to eating from human sources have been known to hit out when denied a meal.

Because of their ability to digest almost anything, marabou droppings are very corrosive to metal. Many homeowners and motorists find this out when the storks roost in towns and their droppings corrode metal roofs!

NILE CROCODILE

The Nile crocodile has a quite deserved repute as a nasty man-eater. The nearness of much of its territory to populaces means confrontations are common. And it's almost undifferentiating fare means a country dweller doing laundry at the waterside might look just as yummy as a wandering gnu.

(Nile crocodile)

Africa's biggest reptilian is the Nile crocodile. These beasts reach an extreme size of about 22 feet. They can weigh up to 1,700 pounds. Nile crocodiles live all over Africa south of the Sahara in mangrove swamps, freshwater marshes, and rivers, and the Nile Basin.

Nile crocodile mainly eats fish. However, it tries to catch almost anything unlucky enough to encounter it, including porcupines, birds, small hippos, wildebeeste, and other crocodiles. It is also a scavenger of dead flesh and, at one feeding, eats up to half its own body.

This terrifying killer has one unusual trait and that is its role as a caring parent. Where most other reptiles lay their eggs and just leave them, parent Nile crocodiles fiercely stand guard near their nests until the eggs hatch. They will often help hatching baby crocs get out of the egg – they take them gently in their mouths and carry them to the water.

They are sometimes hunted and bred for meat and hides – their greenish-yellow underbelly makes high quality, expensive leather.

BLACK MAMBA
(Black mamba)

The black mamba is sometimes called the black-mouthed mamba. It is the lengthiest snake in Africa that is venomous, and grows to and average of around 8.2-10 ft in length, sometimes growing to lengths of more than 14ft. The inside of its mouth is a blue-black color and that's where it gets its name. Its scales which vary from dull greenish-yellow to a metallic grey. When threatened, it displays its blue-black mouth. The black mamba is the fastest snake in the world, and can of move almost as fast as a running man. The black mamba is reputed for being very violent. However, it typically tries to escape from humans like most snakes, unless it is in danger. Without quick and thorough anti-venom treatment, a black mamba's bite is almost always mortal.

The black mamba has a large, tapered and extended coffin-shaped head. It has fixed fangs, located at the front of its mouth. The eyes are black to brownish with a yellowish edge on the pupils. The black mamba has acclimatized to a variety of environments; from savanna, woodlands, farms, rocky inclines, dense woods and humid marshes. The savannah grasslands and woody shrubs that extend cover southern and eastern Africa are the black mamba's usual ground. Black mambas rear young once a year.

Black mambas are wild, jumpy, mortally poisonous, and when vulnerable, highly hostile. They have been attributed for several human deaths, and African mythologies embellish their abilities to legendary magnitudes. For these reasons, the black mamba's label as the world's deadliest snake is well deserved.

The cheetah is a large feline inhabiting most of Africa and parts of the Middle East. No land animal is faster than the cheetah – it can run as fast as 70 to 75 mph in short spurts, and accelerate from 0 to 60 mph in three seconds. This cat is also noteworthy for adaptations in the species' paws. It is one of the few with semi-sheathable claws – most have fully sheathable claws.

The cheetah's chest is deep. It has a narrow waist. Its tan fur has round spots and if coarse and short, giving it camouflage for stalking and hunting. The tail ends in a hairy white clump. The cheetah's small head and eyes that are set high, combined with its thin and streamlined body, are suitable for short bursts of high speed, but not for long-distance running.

Females take about two years to reach maturity, and males take around one year. However, males don't usually mate until at they're least three years old. They mate all through the year. Studies have found that, often, females will have cubs by many different mates.

A cheetah's diet depends on its habitat. On the East African savannah it prefers the Thomson's gazelle. A small antelope which is smaller and slower than the cheetah, it makes an appropriate prey. Individual gazelles which have strayed from the group are the cheetah's main target, rather than old or weak ones.

Eastern and southwestern Africa are the areas where most wild cheetahs are to be found. Only seven to ten thousand of these big cats are believed to remain. Sadly, human settlements continue to put pressure even on these remaining few.

THE LAUGHING HYENA
(Spotted hyena in the Masai Mara National Park, Kenya)

There are three hyena species; spotted, brown and striped, with spotted being the largest. Hyenas are actually more closely related to cats although they appear similar to dogs. Hyenas live all over much of Africa, Arabia and India. They live in "clans". These comprise something like 80 members and are led by alpha females.

Because of increasing population pressure, human-hyena contact is frequent. For instance, in Kenya and Tanzania, the Masai people let hyenas consume their dead. Hyenas are smart and courageous animals and they will raid granaries and farms. They are held to blame for the deaths of many livestock and even some humans. They are sometimes hunted as damaging nuisances.

With good hearing and sharp night vision, hyenas are good hunters. They can run fast and far without tiring. Hyenas work as teams to isolate prey; sometimes an ill or infirm animal, and pursue run it death. The hyenas often squabble over the kill, sometimes among themselves or against other powerful predators like lions. Their jaws are among the most powerful of any animal, capable of crushing even the toughest bones.

Spotted hyenas are very noisy. They make a wide range of vocalizations, including the "laughter" that is associated with their name. Their eyes shining in the dark by the light of a campfire, accompanied by the giggling "laughter" can give you the shivers!

Read More Amazing Animal Books

Website http://AmazingAnimalBooks.com

Join our newsletter and receive

Amazing Animal Fact Sheets and

Get new books to review as soon as they come out

This book is published by

JD-Biz Corp

P O Box 374

Mendon, Utah 84325

http://www.jd-biz.com/

Read more books from John Davidson

Over 500 Books and over 500,000 copies Downloaded